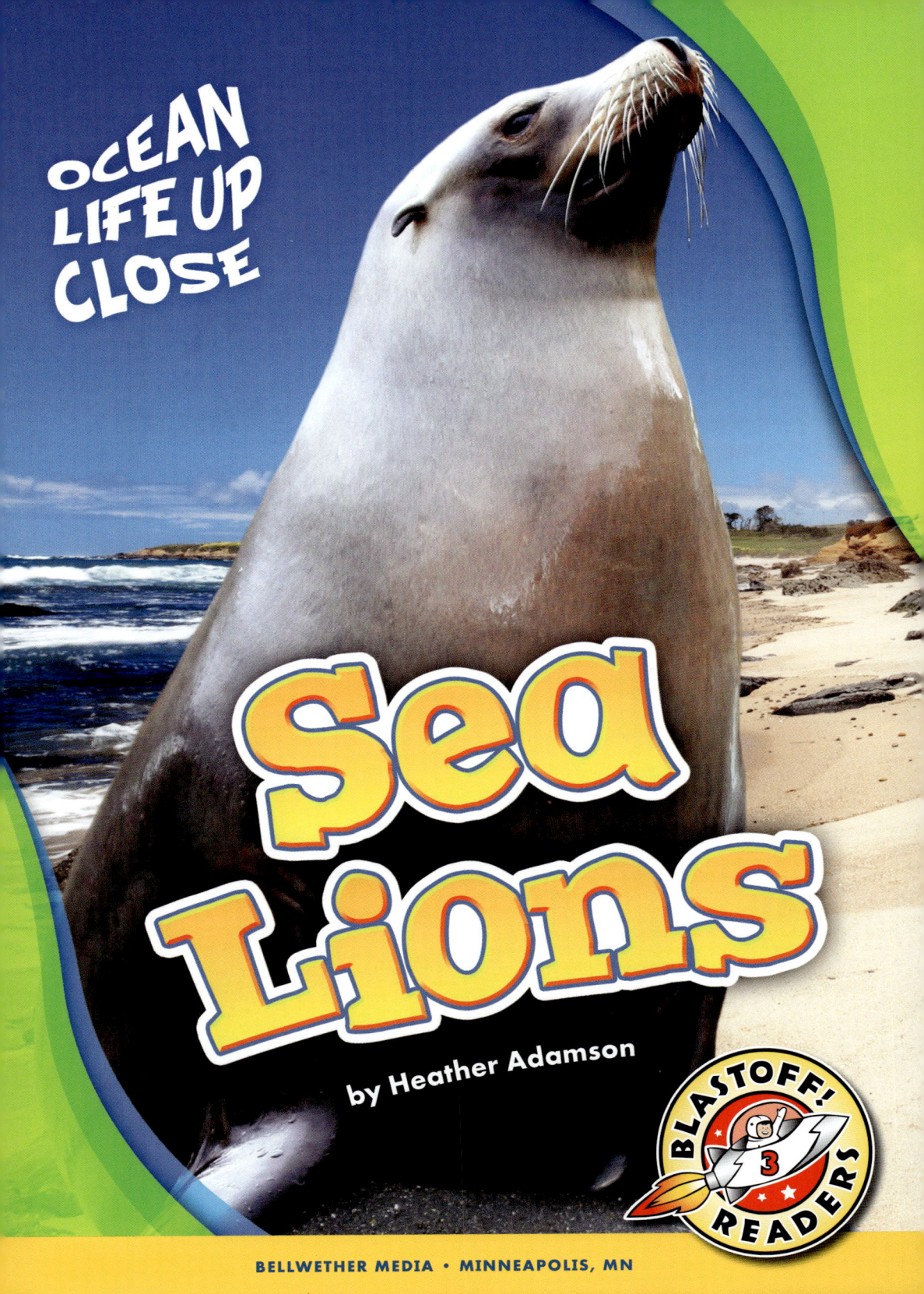

Note to Librarians, Teachers, and Parents:

Blastoff! Readers are carefully developed by literacy experts and combine standards-based content with developmentally appropriate text.

Level 1 provides the most support through repetition of high-frequency words, light text, predictable sentence patterns, and strong visual support.

Level 2 offers early readers a bit more challenge through varied simple sentences, increased text load, and less repetition of high-frequency words.

Level 3 advances early-fluent readers toward fluency through increased text and concept load, less reliance on visuals, longer sentences, and more literary language.

Level 4 builds reading stamina by providing more text per page, increased use of punctuation, greater variation in sentence patterns, and increasingly challenging vocabulary.

Level 5 encourages children to move from "learning to read" to "reading to learn" by providing even more text, varied writing styles, and less familiar topics.

Whichever book is right for your reader, Blastoff! Readers are the perfect books to build confidence and encourage a love of reading that will last a lifetime!

This edition first published in 2018 by Bellwether Media, Inc.

No part of this publication may be reproduced in whole or in part without written permission of the publisher. For information regarding permission, write to Bellwether Media, Inc., Attention: Permissions Department, 5357 Penn Avenue South, Minneapolis, MN 55419.

Library of Congress Cataloging-in-Publication Data

Names: Adamson, Heather, 1974- author.
Title: Sea Lions / by Heather Adamson.
Description: Minneapolis, MN : Bellwether Media, Inc., [2018] | Series: Blastoff! Readers. Ocean Life Up Close | Audience: Ages 5-8. | Audience: K to grade 3. | Includes bibliographical references and index.
Identifiers: LCCN 2016057232 (print) | LCCN 2017019433 (ebook) | ISBN 9781626176454 (hardcover : alk. paper) | ISBN 9781681033754 (ebook)
Subjects: LCSH: Sea lions–Juvenile literature.
Classification: LCC QL737.P63 (ebook) | LCC QL737.P63 A33 2018 (print) | DDC 599.79/75–dc23
LC record available at https://lccn.loc.gov/2016057232

Text copyright © 2018 by Bellwether Media, Inc. BLASTOFF! READERS and associated logos are trademarks and/or registered trademarks of Bellwether Media, Inc. SCHOLASTIC, CHILDREN'S PRESS, and associated logos are trademarks and/or registered trademarks of Scholastic Inc., 557 Broadway, New York, NY 10012.

Editor: Nathan Sommer   Designer: Lois Stanfield

Printed in the United States of America, North Mankato, MN.

Table of Contents

What Are Sea Lions?	4
Fur, Flippers, and Ear Flaps	8
Filling Up on Fish	14
Herd Life	18
Glossary	22
To Learn More	23
Index	24

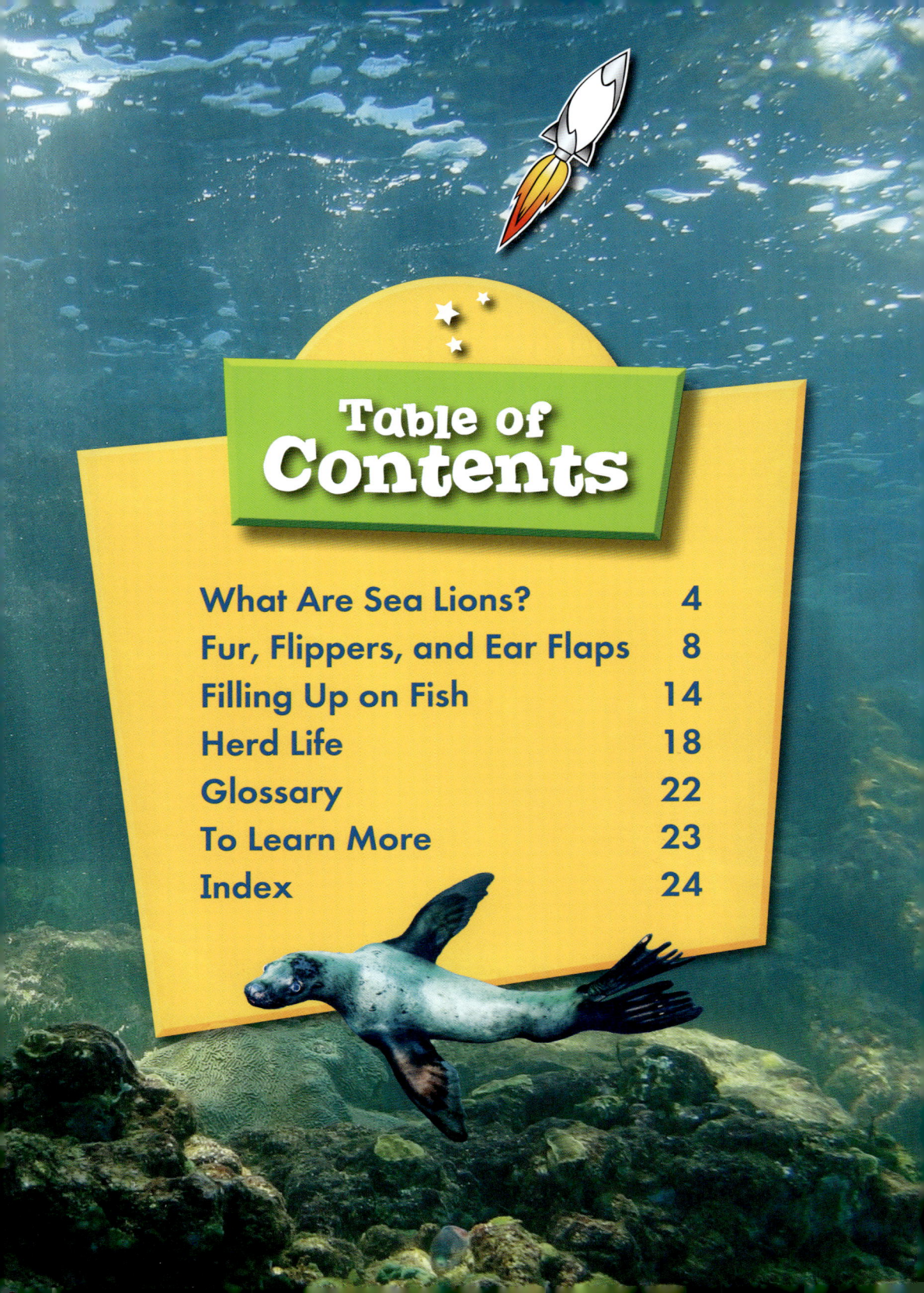

What Are Sea Lions?

Steller sea lions

Sea lions are ocean **mammals** with noisy barks. These **pinnipeds** live along coasts around the world.

Other Pinnipeds
- earless seals
- fur seals
- walruses

Their bodies have layers of thick **blubber**. This keeps them warm in the cold waters where they live.

Species Spotlight
CALIFORNIA SEA LION

life span:
up to 30 years

depth range:
0 to 900 feet
(0 to 274 meters)

California sea lion range =

conservation status: least concern

| Extinct | Extinct in the Wild | Critically Endangered | Endangered | Vulnerable | Near Threatened | Least Concern |

Sea lions live in every ocean except the Atlantic. They like to spend time both on land and in the water.

These creatures often rest in groups on rocky shores and floating docks.

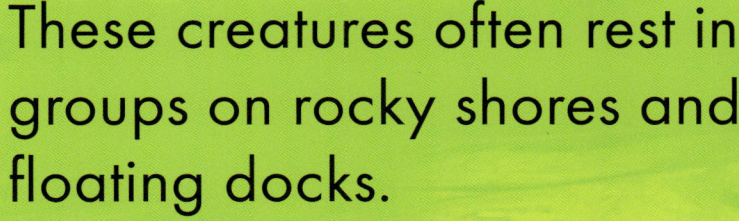

California sea lions

Fur, Flippers, and Ear Flaps

Sea lions have short brown or gray fur. They often look darker when wet.

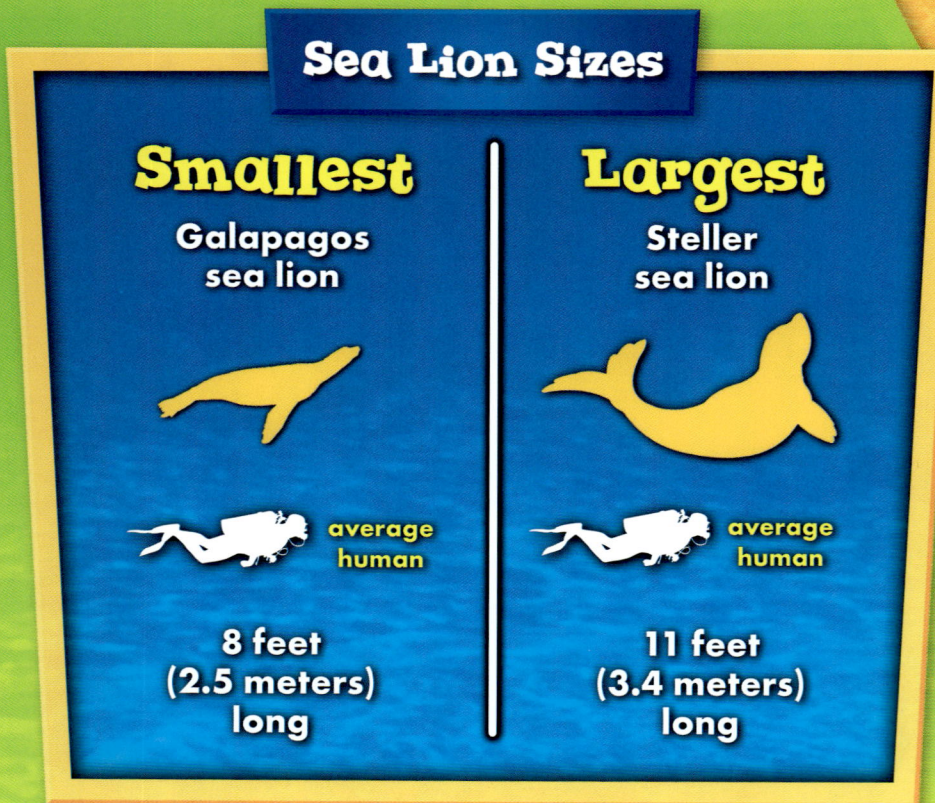

Sea Lion Sizes

Smallest
Galapagos sea lion
average human
8 feet (2.5 meters) long

Largest
Steller sea lion
average human
11 feet (3.4 meters) long

Galapagos sea lion

The biggest sea lions can be 11 feet (3.4 meters) long. They weigh up to 2,400 pounds (1,089 kilograms)!

Sea lions have large, strong **flippers**. They use these to swim in bursts up to 25 miles (40 kilometers) per hour.

flipper

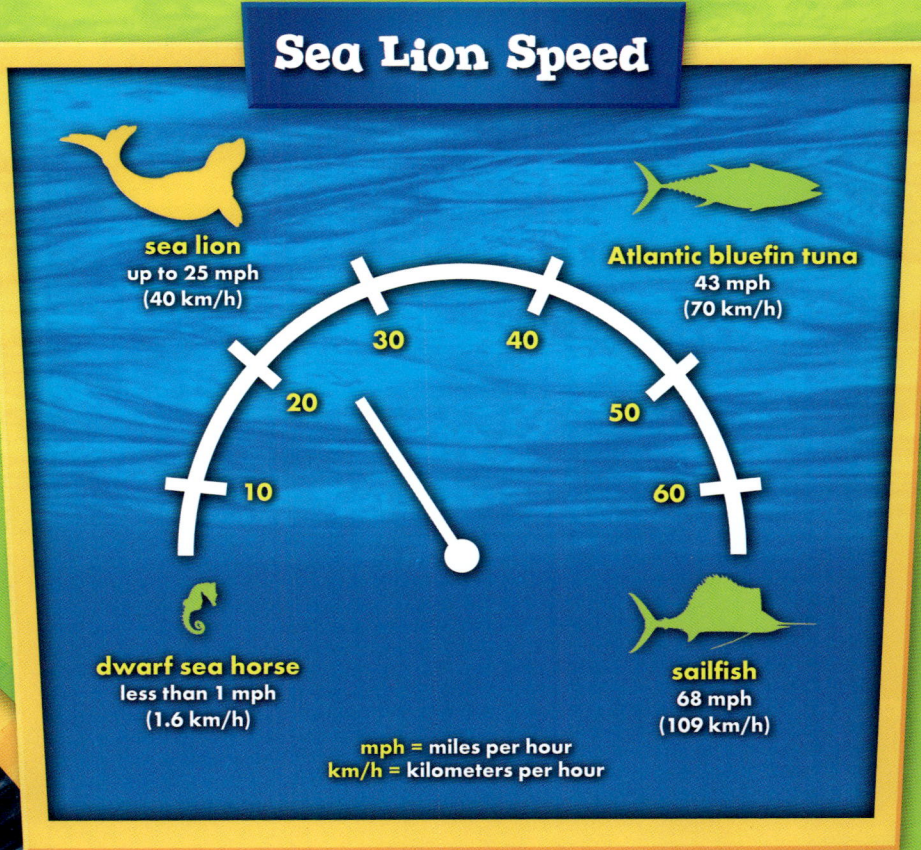

The flippers also act as feet. They help sea lions hold themselves up to walk on land!

Sea lions have **ear flaps** on both sides of their round heads. These keep water out of their ears while they swim.

Whiskers on their faces help sea lions find food. They can sense movement underwater from hundreds of feet away!

Identify a Sea Lion

whiskers

ear flaps

flippers

Filling Up on Fish

Sea lions are not picky eaters. These **carnivores** eat any **prey** they can catch. Anchovies and squid are favorite meals.

Sea lions use their teeth to cut food into big chunks.

Catch of the Day

cuttlefish

Chinook salmon

Dungeness crabs

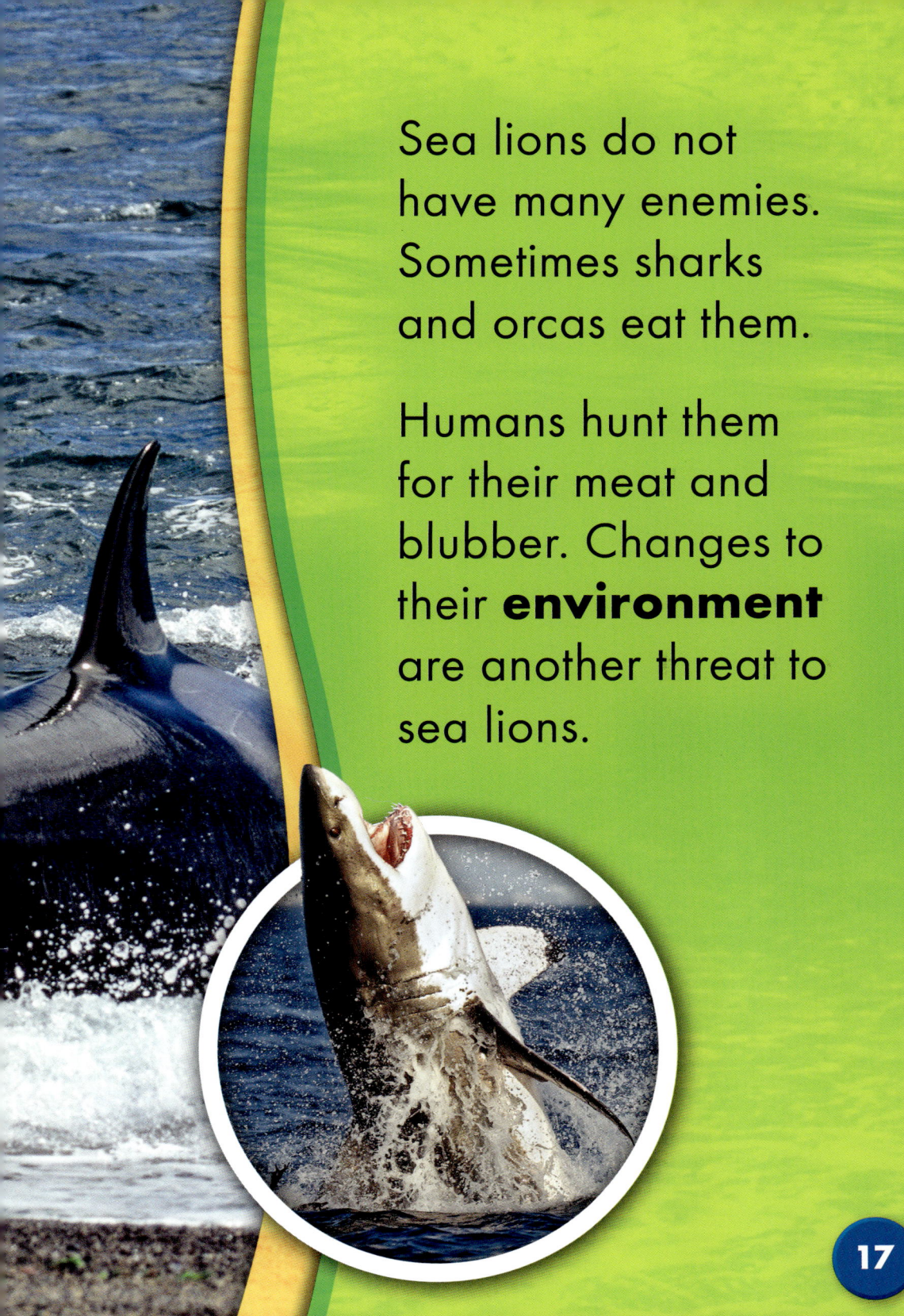

Sea lions do not have many enemies. Sometimes sharks and orcas eat them.

Humans hunt them for their meat and blubber. Changes to their **environment** are another threat to sea lions.

Herd Life

Sea lions get their name from the roaring sounds they make.

herd

They live together in big **herds** that make a lot of noise. These groups often hunt and rest on shore together.

pup

Baby sea lions are called **pups**. Females give birth to one pup at a time.

Pups can swim when they are a few months old. Soon, they will learn how to hunt with mom!

Glossary

blubber—the fat of sea lions

carnivores—animals that only eat meat

ear flaps—flaps of skin and fur that cover a sea lion's ear holes

environment—the natural surroundings of living things

flippers—flat, wide body parts that are used for swimming

herds—groups of sea lions

mammals—warm-blooded animals that have backbones and feed their young milk

pinnipeds—ocean mammals with four flippers; seals, sea lions, and walruses are pinnipeds.

prey—animals that are hunted by other animals for food

pups—baby sea lions

To Learn More

AT THE LIBRARY

Pettiford, Rebecca. *Seals*. Minneapolis, Minn.: Bellwether Media, 2017.

Riggs, Kate. *Sea Lions*. Mankato, Minn.: Creative Education, 2015.

Ryndak, Rob. *Seal or Sea Lion?* New York, N.Y.: Gareth Stevens Publishing, 2016.

ON THE WEB

Learning more about sea lions is as easy as 1, 2, 3.

1. Go to www.factsurfer.com.

2. Enter "sea lions" into the search box.

3. Click the "Surf" button and you will see a list of related web sites.

With factsurfer.com, finding more information is just a click away.

Index

blubber, 5, 17
bodies, 5
carnivores, 14
coasts, 4
colors, 8
depth, 6
docks, 7
ear flaps, 12, 13
enemies, 16, 17
environment, 17
females, 20
flippers, 10, 11, 13
food, 13, 14, 15
fur, 8
heads, 12
herds, 19
hunt, 17, 19, 21
life span, 6
mammals, 4
name, 18
pinnipeds, 4, 5

prey, 14, 15
pups, 20, 21
range, 4, 6
rest, 7, 19
shores, 7, 19
size, 8, 9
sounds, 4, 18, 19
speed, 10, 11
status, 6
swim, 10, 12, 21
teeth, 14
walk, 11
whiskers, 12, 13

The images in this book are reproduced through the courtesy of: Mariusz S. Jurgielewicz, front cover (background); Yair Leibovich, front cover (sea lion); Irmun, pp. 2-3 (background), 22-24; Paul Souders/ Getty Images, pp. 3 (sea lion), 10-11; KenCanning, pp. 4-5, 8-9; Marco Rolleman, p. 5 (top); SkyLynx, p. 5 (center); Vladimir Melnik, p. 5 (bottom); robertharding/ Alamy, p. 6; Arto Hakola, p. 7; Javid Kheyrabadi, p. 8 (Steller sea lion); IURII BURIAK, p. 9; Steve Bloom Images/ Alamy, pp. 12-13; chbaum, p. 13 (top left, top center); Roger de Montfort, p. 13 (bottom, top right); Rich Reid/ Getty Images, p. 14; Alex Mustard/Nature Picture Library/ Getty Images, pp. 14-15; kunanon, p. 15 (left); SNC Art and More, p. 15 (right); Tory Kallman, p. 15 (center); François Gohier / VWPics/ Alamy, pp. 16-17; Andrea Izzotti, p. 16 (left, center); Doug Perrine/ Alamy, p. 16 (right); Sergey Uryadnikov, p. 17; David Gowans/ Alamy, p. 18; Grafissimo, p. 19; Bildagentur Zoonar GmbH, pp. 20-21 (sea lions); EA Given, pp. 20-21 (background); WaterFrame/ Alamy, p. 21.